T0209354

ESSENTIALS

ESSENTIALS

We Can't Live Life Without Them

Mark Stermer

WestBow Press books may be ordered through booksellers or by contacting:

WestBow Press
A Division of Thomas Nelson & Zondervan
1663 Liberty Drive
Bloomington, IN 47403
www.westbowpress.com
844-714-3454

ISBN: 979-8-3850-0637-3 (sc)
ISBN: 979-8-3850-0638-0 (e)

Library of Congress Control Number: 2023916390

Print information available on the last page.

WestBow Press rev. date: 09/07/2023

Contents

Introduction

Your life is important and should be cared for and nurtured. The quality of your life is just as important as life itself. That's why Jesus said, "I came to bring you life and life more abundant!" Well, life and the quality of life hinges first on the essentials of air, water, food, and shelter. Any survivalist or mother would tell you this. Human beings must physically have these four essentials to survive and thrive. Clean air, pure water, healthy food, and adequate shelter are essentials. However, to stop here would be naive and immature. We are not just physical beings. Human beings are made differently than all other creatures on the earth. We have a soul inside of our physical bodies that also has needs, including the need to be cared for and nurtured. Our physical essentials mirror our spiritual essentials. Our spirits also need clean air, pure water, healthy food, and adequate shelter.

I think we would all agree that there are too many people in the world suffering and laboring in unhealthy environments where the air is polluted, the water is contaminated, the food is scarce, and the shelter is inadequate. This should concern us because we are all called to be caretakers of the earth. We all have a responsibility to be good stewards of the manifold blessings of the earth. This started from the beginning when God handed over the keys to Adam and Eve to do just that. That includes helping our fellow human beings who have been ravaged by life or have fallen on hard times to have better lives. After all, the mark of true Christianity is serving and helping the less fortunate on the earth. These four physical essentials must be considered in our quest.

Just as there are too many people in the world suffering and laboring in life from a lack of the physical essentials, there are also too many people in the world suffocating, dehydrating, starving, and suffering exposure in their spirits. I would make the appeal to consider that there are even more spiritually needy people than physically needy people in our world today. Maybe you are one of those in this latter category and you are suffering and laboring to stay alive. Well, I have good news for you! God cares about you both physically and spiritually. He wants to care for you and nurture you not just so you stay alive, but so you find and remain in a flourishing environment where the air is clean, the water is pure, the food is healthy, and the shelter is adequate. He wants you to live in a place where anxiety, fear, lack, struggle, and regret are all but eliminated.

My prayer is that this book will be a tool that our Father and Lord Jesus Christ may use to help you find this place of life and life more abundant. I ask You, Holy Spirit, to bring these pages alive in the heart of every person who would embark on this survivalist journey. Come now and take a deep breath, drink it in, fill your soul, and change your address. It's time. Walk through this open door and experience life in a whole new way.

Chapter 1
Air

Everyone knows a person cannot survive without air. We can survive maybe three minutes without air before bad things begin to happen. Have you ever been in a situation where your air flow was shut off or you couldn't seem to get enough air? Personally, in my opinion, I have had too many of those experiences. In military dive training and water safety survival school, the instructors would put me in scenarios where my air was either cut off or restricted, and evaluate how I reacted.

The whole idea was not to panic. Just do what needed to be done to get the oxygen flowing again. Sometimes that meant untangling a hose or calmly breathing through extreme factors created around me. These exercises proved invaluable in saving my life more than a few times.

Oxygen is not just essential physically, but it can also be looked at as an essential spiritually. In Genesis 2:7 (NASB20) it says, "Then the LORD God formed the man of dust from the ground and breathed into his nostrils the breath of life; and the man became a living person." The Lord God did not just give humans physical breath, but He gave us spiritual breath as well.

Job 34:14–15 (NLT) says, "If God were to take back his spirit and withdraw his breath, all life would cease, and humanity would turn again to dust." This speaks of a continual dependence on the Lord our God to exist. I guess the best earthly example I have is between us and plant life. Without plant life, the air we breathe would not be cleaned and enriched with oxygen, so we could continue to exist. Without continued interaction between us and the Lord, we would cease to exist.

Job 33:4 (NASB 20) reads, "The Spirit of God has made me, And the breath of the Almighty gives me life." One can argue that the air we breathe in is both physical and spiritual—especially for a born-again believer.

Here is something to consider. When someone accepts Jesus Christ as the Son of God, he or she is turned into a new creature. Literally, the Lord our God makes a new species of human being. We are the 2.0 version, born from the second Adam, Jesus Christ.

Look how this happens in John 20:21–22 (NASB20): "So Jesus said to them again, 'Peace be to you; just as the Father has sent Me, I also send you.' And when He had said this, He breathed on them and said to them, 'Receive the Holy Spirit.'" This happened after they believed Jesus Christ had risen from the dead. In the same way our Heavenly Father breathed life physically and spiritually into Adam, the second Adam, Jesus Christ, breathed life into all who believe in Him.

Perhaps this is why the Bible tells us in Revelation 3:1b (NASB 20) that "I know your deeds, that you have a name, that you are alive, and yet you are dead." Jesus also said in another passage to "let the dead bury the dead." He is referring to people physically alive yet spiritually dead. This is because the life-giving breath of Jesus Christ is not flowing through them. However, it is flowing through those of us who have become children of God.

Going back to the example of interaction between plant life and human life, for we who are believers, there is an interaction between us and the Lord, which must happen for us to exist. Just as we naturally breathe in and out to receive the oxygen we need, so too must we find this exercise in the spirit: to breathe in life, and for our Lord to receive our breath back to Himself. This should be an exercise that never ends.

We see a picture of this in Psalm 150:6, which says, "Everything that has breath shall praise the LORD. Praise the LORD."

It is interesting that in heaven, the one activity that never ceases is praise and worship. Praise and worship for us should be as natural as breathing. Praise and worship is not just singing, but living each moment of the day in awe and awareness of the presence of the Spirit of God. I love the song, "This Is the Air I Breathe," which says, "This is the air I breathe / This is the air I breathe / Your holy presence."

When life gets tangled up and you can't breathe, or you find yourself in a scenario where it is hard to breathe, don't panic. Calmly untangle your lifeline by lifting your heart and mind in praise and worship to God. To aid you in breathing, turn on some praise or worship and take a deep spiritual breath. You will be refreshed and filled with the life-giving breath of Jesus Christ.

In this first essential, air, we see that we have been created to praise and worship the Lord God almighty. This needs to be something we do privately, corporately, continually, and sincerely. Praise and worship are not hard, but natural to the one who has had the breath of Jesus Christ breathed into him or her.

Let me give a few tips that will help you.

1. Breathe pure and clean spiritual air.
2. When you come to church, come to participate in praise and worship. Start by being on time and engaging in the moment. Let your spirit reach

out to God and allow your emotions to express your gratitude, love, and devotion.

3. Learn to praise and worship God in your personal and private time with the Lord each day. Use iTunes or nature or both to help you enter. Speak out loud to give honor and glory to the Lord.
4. Live your life to honor and please our Father and Lord Jesus Christ. Keep an awareness of His holy presence all around you.

Chapter 2
Water

Water is another essential. One can only go without water for a few days until weakness, desperation, pain, and eventually death will occur. I remember a time when I was a boy. I went fishing in an out-of-the-way place, which is saying a lot coming from a town that was already out of the way. To get there, I rode my bicycle, while carrying my fishing supplies. It was quite a few miles, as I remember. I rode there early in the morning, fished a few hours, caught some fish, put them on the stringer, and began the long trek back home. I peddled my bike while carrying all my fishing equipment and fish. The problem was I brought no water. Well, this was Louisiana in the summer months with 100 percent humidity. It was hot and dry, so my little venture turned into a not-so-good situation. Here I was, dehydrating with water all around me, but none of it was fit to drink. I was so weak that I couldn't even peddle any longer. I threw away my poor little fish and even jettisoned some of my gear. I was cramping up in pain and close to heat exhaustion. Thank God someone came along, picked me up, gave me some water, and brought me home. I learned a valuable life lesson: drive a car and fish in the cooler months. Haha! No—I learned one must make sure to have water on the journey. We need water; it is essential.

Just as we need physical water, we also need spiritual water. Psalm 42:1–2a says,

"As the deer pants for the water brooks, so my soul pants for You, God. My soul thirsts for God, for the living God." Look, we live in a world that is spiritually dry and humid. If we don't have spiritual water to bring along with us, our experiences will be much like the one I described above, or even worse. Jesus Christ understands our need for spiritual water. We see this in the encounter He has with the woman at the well in John 4. This woman understood the need for physical water, but she was oblivious of her need for spiritual water. Her life was marked with weakness, pain, and desperation. Jesus Christ came along and gave her what she really needed: living water. Like this woman, many people today burden themselves with the heavy loads of physical things. They have to get more, or try their best to satisfy their thirst, only to be disappointed and left stranded on the road. We don't have to live that way. Jesus Christ sent me to you today in the form of this writing to rescue you from this fate.

In Revelation 22:1, John says, "And he showed me a river of the water of life, clear as crystal, coming from the throne of God and of the Lamb." If we drink from this river, it will satisfy our thirst and hydrate us to live life to its fullest. This water will strengthen us to make the journey. I would like to show you what this river really is, how it can exist in your life, and how you can continuously drink from it. There are so many people out there who are thirsty, desperate, and in pain. Maybe you are the one in that place. Well, today I offer you a clear, clean, and pure drink of living water.

Okay, check this out. John 7:37–39a states, "Now on the last day, the great day of the feast, Jesus stood and cried out saying, 'If anyone is thirsty, let him come to Me and drink. The one who believes in Me, as the Scripture said, from his innermost being will flow rivers of living water.' But this He said in reference to the Spirit, whom those who believed in Him were to receive." Now we can see and understand what the living water is. It's the Holy Spirit living inside of us. If you are born again, this water is available to you. The problem is there are so many Christians today who fail to take advantage of what has been given to them. I see so many brothers and sisters in the Lord living in the same desperation as those in the world going to their useless wells. I also see so many of my spiritual family traveling here and there looking for their oases, only to realize they are following mirages. That is why they keep being disappointed in their many destinations and dry wells. You see, the real, satisfying, life-giving water is within you. Stop looking at the water around you because it is unfit to drink and will never satisfy your soul.

"Drink from My river," says the

Lord. We do this by looking within and connecting to the Holy Spirit of God. The Bible says in 2 Corinthians 13:14, "The grace of the Lord Jesus Christ, and the love of God, and the communion of the Holy Spirit be with you all. Amen." To commune with the Holy Spirit is to hydrate your soul for the journey ahead. One of the best ways to do this is through the ancient biblical practice of meditation. Stop, let down your bucket that's tied to a rope in your hands, take a dip of clean, fresh, and pure living water, and pull it back up to your thirsting soul. This is what's available to you. However, it's not just for us, but for us to use on our journeys to give to that person we run into stranded and desperate on the road. When we stop and give the person a drink, we can then take him or her home to Jesus Christ.

Go ahead and find a nice shady place to meditate and connect with the Holy Spirit of God within you. He is waiting to fill you with fresh, clean, clear, and pure life-giving holy water. While you are meditating, don't forget to breathe in and out (i.e. worship). It will greatly enhance the experience and taste of the water.

Let me give you a few tips to help you stay hydrated.

1. Find a quiet place without distractions and comfortably position yourself in an alert but relaxed state. (Biblical meditation was practiced by the fathers of the faith in the Bible.)
2. Start off by closing your eyes and taking deep breaths in and out. Make your mind be in the moment by focusing on your breaths. The goal here is to control your mind and make it listen to you. (The Lord tells us to take every thought captive.)

3. Then slowly return to normal breathing and make your spirit reach out to connect to the Holy Spirit. You will feel a switch in the atmosphere when you start connecting. (The Lord tells us to commune with the Holy Spirit.)
4. Start reflecting on the last twenty-four hours of your life, asking the Holy Spirit to show you how you did in relation to living as the Lord instructs us. In your mind, run through every meeting or encounter you had from the day before. (Just as we see in the example of David, we ask the Lord to search us and help us see when there are things we need to adjust.)
5. Then take some deep breaths again to refocus your mind. Direct your mind to the day you are about to live. I look in my calendar to see what is scheduled, then I meditate

through each perceived upcoming meeting, asking the Holy Spirit to show me anything I might need and to prepare the way. (The Lord tells us that the Helper will show us things to come and even show us deep things. He also tells us that He goes before us.)

6. Again, take deep breaths to center your mind and refocus it on the Holy Spirit. Then ask the Holy Spirit to take you to wherever He wants or to show you whatever He knows you need to see. Then allow your mind to follow Him wherever He wants to bring it. You will be amazed by where He brings you and to whom He directs you. He will show you a picture of something, a person or something about your life that will help you with work, relationships, or kingdom purposes. When He does, jot them down and ask for His help.

(The Holy Spirit is called the Helper for a reason.)

7. Center your mind once more, then go deep inside your feelings and be honest with what you find. At this point, you can write those down, making sure to involve the Holy Spirit so that He can help you find truth, solutions, and healing. This exercise is called expressive writing and should be done at least four times a week. (The Lord tells us to examine ourselves so that we can deal with ourselves according to Him.)
8. Slowly come back by taking deep breaths to center your mind to step out into the day.

Do this at least once a day and watch how hydrated you will become.

Note: Go to The Church International App and access Ancient Biblical Practices to learn more about the five pillars of spending time with our Father, Lord, and Helper. There is a specific video on meditation that will also help you drink of the Spirit.

Chapter 3
Food

This is one of my favorite topics. I love good food. The older I have become, the more selective I have become when it comes to eating. It used to be that I would eat anything. It really did not matter what it was as long as it filled my belly. That is not true today. I eat because I need it and because I enjoy it. I also pay attention now to the health benefits of what I am eating. You know the old adage "we are what we eat." Living in Louisiana, food is especially important to our culture. Have you ever noticed that pretty much everything we do is surrounded around food? When someone is coming over, we cook. When someone visits, we offer food. Weddings and funerals have food. After church, we serve food. When we get up, we eat food. Before we go to bed, we eat food—food, food, and more food! Even after we eat dinner, we all move to the living room to do what? Eat more food in the form of dessert. Anyone getting hungry from reading this yet? We can all understand the importance of food and that it is an essential. We, as human beings, can survive about forty days without food before the body enters into starvation and then death. We must have food to live. For most of us, we eat three to four times a day; for some of us, we are on a "see-food" diet. When we see food, we eat it.

Well, food is not just essential physically; it is also essential spiritually. After going without food for forty days, Jesus Christ was tempted to use His power to turn rocks into food, but refused to do so. He rebuked the devil by telling him that people don't live by physical food alone, but by the spiritual food that comes from the mouth of God. I paraphrased this scripture in Matthew 4:4 so that we can better understand how important the word of God is to our lives. Jesus Christ says that spiritual food is even more important than physical food. Yes, physical food is important, but it is not what we should live our lives for. It should not be the object of our pursuits. In another story, the people sought Jesus Christ not because they wanted to hear the word of God from Him, but because of the physical food He supernaturally provided for them earlier. They valued the natural food over the spiritual food. Jesus Christ understands we need natural food, but it should never be the object of our pursuits. Jesus Christ tells us to put the spiritual first and the natural will be there when we need it (Matthew 6). Are we more in love with the physical food than we are with the spiritual food? Do some of us seek after Jesus only for the physical benefits or also for the spiritual benefits? If we wish to be healthy and strong in life, we should obsess over the spiritual food not the natural food. We are told in many places in the scripture to meditate on the word of God night and day. This means to make our pursuit spiritual then the natural will be taken care of.

Here is something very important to understand about the spiritual food we need to survive and to be healthy as spiritual beings. In Matthew 4:4, the Greek word used for *word* is *rhema*. *Rhema* means personal revelation. Merely reading the word of God will not feed your spirit. You must have a personal revelation of the meaning from the word of God for it to bring the nutrition your soul desires.

For this to happen, our Lord made us into new creatures who have been given special spiritual digestive systems to be able to process His spiritual food upon salvation. That is why someone who is not saved finds no soulish value in eating the word of God. However, even as Christians, we can swallow our spiritual food down the wrong hole if we are not careful. When feeding ourselves this spiritual food, let us open our spiritual mouths to really get the full benefit of the meal. Yes, just as we have physical ears, eyes, and mouths, so do we have spiritual ones. Remember, the Holy Spirit is there to help you wash it down. He or she who has eyes to see, reads, and he or she who has a mouth to open, eats. Here is a good example. Ezekiel 3:1–3 says, "Then He said to me, 'Son of man, eat what you find; eat this scroll, and go, speak to the house of Israel.' So I opened my mouth, and He fed me this scroll. And He said to me, 'Son of man, feed your stomach and fill your body with this scroll which I am giving you.' Then I ate it, and it was as sweet as honey in my mouth."

Wow! That is an awesome picture of what we should be doing each day. I want to encourage you to begin the habit of reading the Bible each day. We have an amazing tool to guide you on your new diet plan, The Ancient Paths Devotional, which is free to you on The Church International App. You can also have it emailed to you each morning by signing up online. Studies show that if you read the word of God in this manner more than four days a week, your life will be significantly better. You will be healthy and strong. Come on in and eat with us. The Bible is the best restaurant in town. It has the best menu and the food is super healthy, but it tastes amazing. Remember, we are what we eat.

Hang on—we are not finished eating.

The problem is that this is where most Christians get up from the table and stop. In doing so, they miss so much. This reminds me of a story of when I was in the military. My friends and I were invited to eat at a stranger's house in Italy. We were so excited to experience Italian culture. We had one slight challenge: the family did not speak English and we did not speak Italian. This was no problem because food was our international language that night. We arrived and the experience began. They brought in some appetizers that were Italian and very delicious. I could not name what they were, but "oui-oui" they were good. You are talking about feeding some very hungry Marines who had been eating ship food for weeks. Then they brought in the pizza. Remember, we were in Italy. This was not Domino's or Pizza Hut pizza. To say the least, we munched down. We ate and ate until they ran out of pizza. We asked for more, so one of the family members left and returned in about thirty minutes with more pizza. After we stuffed ourselves with as much pizza as we could eat, we sat there satisfied and excited about the little adventure. Then something unexpected happened. All of a sudden, our host walked out (with some family members helping him) carrying an amazing feast of lamb, green beans, carrots, and rice. They set it on the table and we all looked at each other and laughed as we realized what had just happened. To be honest, we tried to honor our host by eating the main course, but we were all too full to really enjoy the incredible meal provided for us. This is exactly what happens with many Christians who understand and love the "heavenly" pizza. They sit down, eat, and eat until they are full. They are then ready to get up and leave, satisfied with the experience, but unaware that there is so much more God has for them to eat.

Let me show you what I am talking about. In John 4, Jesus and the disciples had gone quite some time without food. Jesus had sent His disciples to find food and bring it back. He stayed back and ventured to Jacob's well nearby. There He met a Samaritan woman and shared salvation with her. She was floored and ran off to tell the city that she had an encounter with the Messiah. In the meantime, the disciples made their way back to where Jesus was. They witnessed the back end of this encounter. As John 4:31–34 records,

> Meanwhile the disciples were urging Him, saying, "Rabbi, eat something." But He said to them, "I have food to eat that you do not know about." So the disciples were saying to one another, "No one brought Him anything to eat, did he?" Jesus

> said to them, "My food is to do
> the will of Him who sent Me,
> and to accomplish His work."

Wow, here it is! This is the main course many miss, as did the disciples in this story. It is to reach the lost, hear their stories, tell our stories, and stir in the story of the cross on top of it all. Our souls and the people we are sharing it with can be most satisfied with this food. Jesus Christ said, "My food is to do the will of Him who sent Me, and to accomplish His work." What is God's will? It is that all would come to the knowledge of Jesus Christ and be saved (1 Tim. 2:4). What is the work? The work of God is to get people to believe in Jesus Christ as the Son of God (John 6:29).

What the Lord is trying to show us is that if all we do is eat the word, but fail to dine on the mission, we miss out on so much. This is why I see so many Christians serve in church, read their

Bibles, yet remain unsatisfied. It is because they are not sharing their faith with others. Sharing our faith and personally convincing people to believe in Jesus Christ as the Son of God is essential to our spiritual diets. We must be in the word each day, but we also must be sharing that word with others if we desire to be fully nourished and satisfied in our walk with Jesus Christ.

Let me give you a few etiquette tips for your dining experience.

1. Read the Holy Word every day. Studies have shown that if you do this, your life will be significantly better. Use tools like our Ancient Paths Devotional to help you stay consistent and read the entire Bible. This will keep you eating a balanced meal.
2. Don't just read, but ask the Holy Spirit to help you understand and

digest what you are reading. I have my journal next to me when I read and I write down what stands out to me as I am reading. This really helps you get the full value of the meal.

3. Don't stop with reading, but look for opportunities to share your faith with others. This will really bring your experience of Christianity to the next level and it will keep you strong, fresh, and satisfied in your walk.

Chapter 4
Shelter

One of the biggest investments we make in our lives is for shelter. We buy homes for places of rest, protection, and life. Cindy and I love our home. I know many people who seek to escape their homes as often as possible, but Cindy and I look for reasons to be at home. We do staycations, we have many of our dates at home, and we do much of our work from home. Our home is a place for family and a place of hospitality for friends and strangers alike. We love opening our home to be enjoyed by others.

When our home flooded and we lost it for a season, we realized how important a home is to our mental, emotional, and spiritual health. In the world today, there are so many people who are without homes of their own. Many are homeless and others are in rentals. While renting after we flooded, we learned that it does not have the same feel as owning. Don't get me wrong, we were very appreciative to not have to live without a shelter, but we noticed a renter's mentality is very different from an owner's mentality. It felt different mentally and emotionally. For those of you out there who have never been able to own your own home, my heart goes out to you and I hope you are able to do so one day. Not only is it a smart investment, but it is a healthier one, too. In the meantime, I pray for God's grace and mercy to rest on your situation until you, too, can own your own home.

Just as it is healthier to have physical

homes, we also need spiritual homes in our lives. We are shown in the scriptures that we should make God our shelters and our resting places. In Psalm 61:4, it says, "Let me dwell in Your tent forever, let me take refuge in the shelter of Your wings." Psalm 91:1 says, "He who dwells in the shelter of the Most High will abide in the shadow of the Almighty." We are told in the scriptures that if we are planted in the house of the Lord, we will flourish. Even in the famous Psalm 23, the ultimate conclusion of making the Lord our shelter and shepherd was that we could live in the house of the Lord forever. There is a spiritual house that God wants you to live in. This is a house not made with hands, a house that you own because you are an heir, a house built on a foundation that is solid. You are literally and spiritually a part of the building. In 1 Peter 2:5, we are told that we are living stones being built into God's spiritual house.

This spiritual house is the most expensive house ever built and the greatest investment ever made. Jesus Christ paid it all to build this house. Jesus Christ said, "I will build my house!" When we are saved, we become a part of this house. We must invest in this house by having hearts to continue to build with our Lord as children of the house. When we understand that we, too, are owners, we move from a renter's mentality to an owner's care. We were once spiritually homeless and some of us were just renters, but now we are owners and have places to call home—places of rest, protection, life, family, and hospitality for friends and strangers alike.

The Lord has given us the keys to His house. There is no reason for anyone to be homeless. There is plenty of room for anyone who wishes to live here. Do not come in as a renter, but buy into it as an owner. The price to buy in as part owner is offering the Lord Jesus Christ your life. If you wish to be healthy mentally, emotionally, and spiritually, then it is essential for you to buy in. Our Heavenly Father says, "My house shall be called a house of prayer." Well, I pray that the Spirit of the Lord will give you ears to hear and a heart to belong to the house of God.

As you can see, the house of God is the people gathered in the name of Jesus. The house of God is universal, but it is made more accessible to us in a local expression called the local church. The local organized church was and is God's idea. The whole New Testament is not just about getting into God's Kingdom, but also how to live in God's house through the gathering of believers. The New Testament writings were addressed to local churches that were set up by God. In the book of Revelation, Jesus Christ did not visit someone's house or address instructions to one individual; He visited each local church and gave instructions to each body unique to that local expression. The New Testament also sets up leadership for each local church and even calls it fathering and mothering the people (1 and 2 Timothy, Titus, 1 Thessalonians 2). The local church is more than an organization; it is a family of believers working with the rest of the families of believers around the world to reach the lost, train the saved, and serve the poor. Belonging to a local church is an essential part of Christianity. We shouldn't just visit. We shouldn't have a renter's mentality. We should have an owner's heart as a child of God who is an heir to the Kingdom.

Let me give you some house guidance so that you can settle in comfortably.

1. You need to be committed to a local church. Ask the Holy Spirit to guide you to the church He desires you to

be at and commit to that church by attending each week.

2. Willingly submit to the leadership God has set up at that church and remember they are not perfect. Neither are the people in the church, and neither are you. Have bold love and high grace for each other.
3. Take ownership by becoming involved in connect groups and even serving somewhere. Be a giver to your local church through your tithe and offerings. (Read my book *Giving, Tithing and Generosity*.)

Conclusion

In conclusion, it is essential as Christians that we are worshiping, communing, and being led by the Spirit. It is essential that we are daily in the word of God, share our faith with others, and commit to the local church. Just as air, water, food, and shelter are to our physical bodies, so are these things to our spiritual selves. Start breathing in the fresh air, drinking the clean water, eating all the good food, and living in the best house.

Pastor Mark Stermer
About the Author

Mark Stermer is the founder and Senior Pastor of The Church International, a multi-campus church operating around the world through local churches, orphanages, and children's care points. He is the founder and President of Life House University, a 501C3 organization which operates multiple men's and women's homes serving hundreds of precious people in Alabama and Louisiana. He is president and overseer of The Church Academy, which educates children to walk in the ways of

Jesus Christ. He has authored many books and developed many resources that can be found on The Church App. You can also gain access to so much more on the various websites: TheChurch.fm, TheLifeHouse.fm and TheChurchAcademy.fm. He is married to Cindy Stermer and they have eight children, two daughters-in-law, three sons-in-law, and eight grandchildren at present. He also served in the United States Marines as a force reconnaissance Marine. His life mission and reason for doing what he does is to be a world-changer to the glory of God the Father and the Lord Jesus Christ.